PRIMARY SOURCES OF POLITICAL SYSTEMS™

COMMUNISM
A PRIMARY SOURCE ANALYSIS

THEODORE LINK

rosen central
Primary Source™

The Rosen Publishing Group, Inc., New York

Published in 2005 by The Rosen Publishing Group, Inc.
29 East 21st Street, New York, NY 10010

Copyright © 2005 by The Rosen Publishing Group, Inc.

First Edition

Library of Congress Cataloging-in-Publication Data

Theodore Link.
Communism : a primary source analysis / Theodore Link. — 1st ed.
     p. cm. — (Primary sources of political systems)
Includes bibliographical references and index.
Contents: The roots of communism — The emerging communists — A growing
international movement — The Bolshevik Revolution — Soviet power and Asian
communism — The spread of communism — The decline of communism.
ISBN 0-8239-4517-0 (libr. binding)
1. Communism—Juvenile literature. [1. Communism. 2. World politics.]
I. Title. II. Series.
HX73.P678 2003
335.43—dc22
                                                                2003015887

Manufactured in the United States of America

On the cover: Vladimir Lenin addresses a crowd in St. Petersburg, Russia, in
March 1917 during the Russian Revolution.

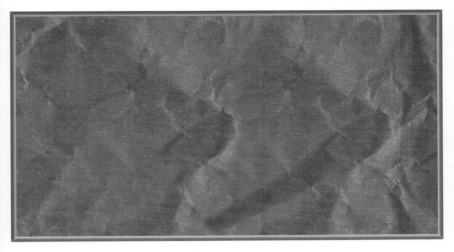

CONTENTS

INTRODUCTION

Communism is defined as a system of government in which citizens share property and labor. However, throughout history, the concept of Communism has meant many different things to many different people. The ancient Greeks viewed it as an ideal vision for the future. Nineteenth-century workers hoped that Communism could better their harsh lives. Idealistic leaders of the early twentieth century aimed to start a revolution that could change the world.

Others feared Communism's ideas. Americans despised the concept of limiting private property. Europeans worried that the powerful USSR and other Communist nations would take over their governments.

During the twentieth century, Communism rose, then fell, in part because of economic pressures brought about by the United States. The Communist system failed because it became oppressive, with brutal dictators controlling their states. Equality was achieved, but only an equality of poverty. Corruption marred the distribution of goods, which was supposed to make citizens equal. Communism changed the world, but the Communist revolution failed.

Chairman Mao Tse-tung *(second from left)* of China reviews an honor guard upon his arrival at the Moscow airport in 1957. He is accompanied by the Soviet chief of staff Marshall Kliment Yefremovich Voroshilov. The USSR and China were powerful Communist allies.

CHAPTER ONE

THE ROOTS OF COMMUNISM

The concept of Communism has existed for thousands of years. The ancient Greeks, who invented democracy, also envisioned a time called the Golden Age. In the Golden Age, people would live together in peace and harmony with no sense of private property. This was a form of Communism.

The *Republic* and Religious Orders

The Greek philosopher Plato (c. 428–347 BC) outlined his own ideas for a perfect government in a work called *Republic*, which was written as a dialogue led by the great teacher Socrates. Plato

This portrait of Robert Owen was created around 1810. Owen was one of the three men considered to be the primary forerunners of modern Communist thought.

intended *Republic* to teach his students about justice. *Republic*'s characters proposed a society ruled by wise thinkers called philosopher-kings.

In *Republic*, an elite group of educated warriors called guardians protect their imagined city. The city provides all citizens with ample food, clothing, and shelter. The guardians share family responsibilities, homes, and food. Private property stops existing for the guardians. They become more capable defenders when freed from these distractions. Everyone happily serves the city's needs. Communal property ensures that the philosopher-kings rule the city for the interests of the people, not to serve their own greed. Plato's dream city never came to exist, but the influence of his ideas grew.

There are many examples of societies based on communal living throughout history. An early Jewish order called the Essenes believed in a highly organized society based on shared property. They viewed trade as evil. Throughout Europe, religious orders took up the notion of communal living. Early Christian groups such as the Gnostics and Manichaeans believed that private property was evil and that the whole earth was for the use of all people. More communal orders arose as Christianity spread. In the Americas, the Incas built an empire based on the idea of communal property and labor.

The Birth of Utopianism

As Europe came into the Middle Ages, a form of government called the manorial system evolved. The Middle Ages, lasting from 400 to 1499, marked a general decline in European society. Under the manorial system, landlords owned the land and peasants worked the fields.

This fifteenth-century painting depicts peasants working in the shadows of a magnificent castle. Under the feudal system, the lower classes were usually taxed more than the higher classes.

Much of the yield from the harvest went to the landlord as rent. The peasants worked the land together to lessen the burden on each person. Villages often contained a plot of land called the commons. Every community member worked in the commons, and the food grown there belonged to all who shared the labor. The lords and nobles sometimes tried to take over village commons, but the peasants resisted. They were willing to fight for this common land. Conflicts led to the Peasants' Revolt in England in 1381 and the Peasants' War in Germany during the sixteenth century.

In 1516, a writer and advisor to England's King Henry VIII named Sir Thomas More published a book called *Utopia*. In it, More imagined himself traveling to the nation of Utopia as an ambassador for Henry VIII. There, he and his companions witnessed a society that organized everything in the best interests of humanity.

People who read or heard *Utopia* read aloud were excited by the idea that the Utopians did not have to work constantly. Utopians did not "wear themselves out with perpetual toil, from morning to night, as if they were beasts of burden." Instead, they divided the day and night into twenty-four hours, only six of which were dedicated to work. The rest of their time was devoted to eating, sleeping, and "proper exercise," which usually meant reading or attending lectures. Also, the Utopians had plenty of food and clothing. Their production was greater because all women and men shared the burden of labor.

More imagined that a society similar to Utopia could succeed if everyone was willing to work. The Utopians wore clothing that they made themselves and did not care about accumulating wealth. They had much in common with Plato's guardians in terms of property and division of labor. However, More believed in keeping

This woodcut, entitled *The Island of Utopia*, appeared as an illustration in the third edition of Sir Thomas More's *Utopia*. It depicts the fictional island of Utopia as More might have imagined it. It was created in 1518 by Ambrosius Holbein, a German artist.

distinct family units whole. Plato wanted every citizen to be every other citizen's parent or sibling.

In More's book, citizens govern Utopia democratically. Thirty families elect an official, called a philarch, to govern them. Every ten philarchs select an archphilarch to rule over them. The people in each of the four sections of a Utopian city choose a candidate for the office of prince. All 200 philarchs elect a prince, the highest authority of the city, from these four candidates. All officials have term limits, except for the prince, who rules for life, unless he is removed upon suspicion of planning to enslave the people.

Sir Thomas More never attempted to establish a society like the one he described in his book, but the idea intrigued many others. Other authors wrote similar books. The word "utopia" eventually came to mean any idealistic community.

Industrialization and Utopias

Later thinkers tried to bring More's ideas to life. In the early 1800s, a British man named Robert Owen made an ambitious attempt to start a utopian community.

When the Industrial Revolution began in Great Britain during the eighteenth century, people crowded into cities to find jobs in factories. They often worked long hours in miserable conditions for little pay. The large number of people looking for jobs enabled factory owners to hire people for low wages and fire them when they pleased. Many people suffered sickness and injury caused by poor working conditions.

A manufacturer himself, Owen bought several mills in Scotland. He built communities around them for his workers, complete with good housing and sanitation, schools, and stores. The earnings from the stores were reinvested into the community. Production at his mills increased along with the quality of life enjoyed by his workers. Owen also founded utopian communities in the United States. The most famous of these was New Harmony in Indiana. The communities failed when Owen and his partners disagreed over their management.

Back in Great Britain, Owen helped to pass a workers' rights law in 1819, slightly improving working conditions. Many of Owen's early ideas were outlined in his collection of essays, *A New View of Society*. In them, he outlined what he saw as a novel way to improve the lives of workers everywhere. The cornerstone of Owen's early thought was education. He wrote:

Train any population rationally, and they will be rational. Furnish honest and useful employments to those so trained, and such employments they will greatly prefer to dishonest or injurious occupations.

Owen felt that everyone needed an education. Not only should the government provide education, it should also help unemployed workers by "preparing a reserve of employment for the surplus working classes, when the general demand for labour throughout the country is not equal to the full occupation of the whole." Later in life, Owen worked to start labor unions. By joining together, workers could lobby for improvements in working conditions for their fellow union members.

CHAPTER TWO

THE EMERGING COMMUNISTS

The ideas of the utopian thinkers gave rise to Socialism. Under Socialism, people within a society would gather in communes to share property and responsibilities. Owen envisioned the world peacefully making the transition to his form of Socialism by following the example of his communities. He dreamed of workers coming together in their cooperatives. Wealthy capitalists would no longer own all of the factories and land. Instead, the workers would become joint owners. Communists shared many views with Socialists, but they felt that governments could only make the transition through revolution.

Karl Marx is considered the main architect of modern Communism. His writings continue to be a main source of reference for Communists and Socialists throughout the world. This poster, bearing his image and a quote from *The Communist Manifesto*, was issued by the Socialist Labor Party in the United States between 1965 and 1980.

Communists reacted to a social system divided into classes. The bourgeoisie were the middle-class capitalists who owned the means of production. Below them were the petite bourgeoisie. These were shopkeepers, tradesmen, artisans, and peasants who made money by providing the goods necessary for life and comfort. The bottom rung was made up of the proletariat, the group of poor people who owned no property. The proletariat worked for the bourgeoisie in factories.

The Father of European Communism

François Babeuf is often recognized as the father of Communism in Europe. He emerged after the French Revolution overthrew King Louis XVI and brought democracy to France. In *Manifesto of the Equals*, published in 1796, he argued that the French Revolution had not gone far enough in creating political equality. Babeuf believed that all people should be economic equals. He argued that private property caused people to organize into a society of masters and slaves. His society of equals would divide property evenly. If something could not be divided, then it would be banned.

Babeuf spent time in prison for his writings. He later formed a secret society that plotted to overthrow the government. He was executed in 1797 when his plot was discovered.

The Communist Manifesto

Karl Marx and Friedrich Engels took inspiration from both Robert Owen's social communes and François Babeuf's vision of

Before Karl Marx *(left)* collaborated with Friedrich Engels *(right)* on *The Communist Manifesto*, he published and edited a journal called *Franco-German Annals*, for which Engels wrote many essays. After Marx's death in 1883, Engels edited *Das Kapital*, which was another of Marx's masterpieces.

a proletariat uprising. Born into a middle-class family in Germany, Karl Marx studied law briefly before switching to philosophy. He worked as a journalist writing Socialist commentary until he moved to Paris in 1843. There, he met Friedrich Engels, the son of a wealthy English manufacturer. Engels had become a Socialist after observing the horrible working conditions at his father's factories. Together, they began working on ideas that would later become the basis for modern Communism.

Exiled from Paris in 1845, Marx traveled to Belgium. He joined with a group of artisans who called themselves the Communist League. In 1847, the Communist League was plotting a workers' revolution. The members commissioned Marx and Engels to write an article detailing their goals and beliefs. Marx and Engels began working on *The Communist Manifesto*.

In the opening lines of *The Communist Manifesto*, Marx declared that Europe's ruling powers saw Communism as a threat: "A spectre is haunting Europe—the spectre of Communism. All the powers of old Europe have entered into a holy alliance to exorcise this spectre." Marx then described history as a sequence of class struggles. He wrote: "Society as a whole is more and more splitting up into two great hostile camps, into two great classes directly facing each other—bourgeoisie and proletariat."

To Marx, the Industrial Revolution caused the evolution of the two classes. Factory owners gained profits by spending as little as possible on production and selling more of the finished product.

Before the Industrial Revolution, independent craftsmen and guild members earned a living by selling carefully handcrafted items. This changed after the colonization of the New World and the rise of factories. Goods had to be produced much faster to be sent to the colonies. Instead of a craftsman creating a single piece, many unskilled workers contributed to the finished product. Production sped up with many people performing one task they knew well on many items.

PRICE TWOPENCE.

MANIFESTO

OF THE

COMMUNIST PARTY,

By KARL MARX, and FREDERICK ENGELS.

Authorized English Translation.

EDITED AND ANNOTATED BY FREDERICK ENGELS,
1888.

London:
WILLIAM REEVES, 185, FLEET STREET, E.C.

The Communist Manifesto has been printed in numerous languages since its first publication. Pictured here is the first authorized English translation, which was published in London, England, in 1888. Refer to page 57 for a partial transcription.

The wages of the unskilled factory workers were much lower than those of the skilled craftsmen. The craftsmen charged more for labor because they knew how to produce the entire item. Factory workers knew only how to do one part. Marx described the relationship between the bourgeoisie and the proletariat as one of exploitation. He blasted the bourgeoisie for turning most of society into wage earners with no choice but to serve the existing system. "The bourgeoisie has stripped of its halo every occupation hitherto honoured and looked up to with reverent awe. It has converted the priest, the poet, the man of science, into its paid wage labourers," he wrote.

Marx condemned the effects of factory labor on the worker. He compared wage laborers to an army serving a hierarchy of managers, calling them slaves of the bourgeoisie.

According to Marx, the petite bourgeoisie also resisted the wealthier factory owners "to save from extinction their existence as fractions of the middle class." The petit bourgeoisie only struggled against the bourgeoisie because they did not want to slip into the lower-class proletariat. "They thus defend not their present but their future interests; they desert their own standpoint to adopt that of the proletariat," Marx wrote.

Communists, History, and Revolution

According to *The Communist Manifesto*, the proletariat could only free itself from its position of servitude to the bourgeoisie through revolution. In its greed for money, the middle class created a class of dependent wage earners much larger than itself. "What the bourgeoisie, therefore, produces above all are its own grave-diggers. Its fall and the victory of the proletariat are equally inevitable," wrote Marx.

Marx proposed that the Communist Party take a position of leadership in this revolution and create an international movement. The aim of the proletariat revolution was to erase social classes.

A first step toward this new equality would be the banning of private property. Critics of Communism claimed that taking away or dividing hard-earned property was unjust. Marx replied that wage labor did not create property for the workers, but only capital.

The wage laborer had nothing to exchange for property except work time. Under the system dominated by the bourgeoisie, workers' time became capital, paid regularly. The capital allowed the laborer the means of subsistence only. Workers did not earn enough capital to buy property, and they did not have the time to work toward bettering their position. Accordingly, Marx wrote, few people really had private property at all.

Critics raised concerns that a Communist government would eliminate education and the institution of the family. Marx replied that it would end the exploitation of children by their parents and the influence of the bourgeoisie over education. Under the bourgeois system, children worked in factories and were "transformed into simple articles of commerce and instruments of labour." Marx's Communist government would destroy all divisions of labor. Every worker would be educated in many different kinds of work. As workers took control of governments and the old social order was toppled, even national boundaries would gradually vanish.

Marx addressed the system of classes that placed the bourgeoisie at the top of the social order and the proletariat at the bottom. Throughout history, social classes have struggled against each other. These struggles always ended in the dominance of one class over another. Over time, the new social order would be overturned and another one would rise in its place.

Communism would end the cycle by creating a classless society. Marx finished *The Communist Manifesto* with strong words of encouragement for Communists and workers everywhere: "Let the ruling classes tremble at a Communist revolution. The proletarians have nothing to lose but their chains. They have a world to win. Workingmen of all countries, unite!"

A Growing International Movement

The revolutions foretold by Marx and Engels began all across Europe in 1848, but they all encountered problems. Little coordination existed between the revolutionary groups. Most national armies remained loyal to their old rulers and easily put down the revolts. Marx himself was tried for treason. Acquitted, he was expelled from Prussia, a large influential state in north-central Germany. The next two decades saw Communism dwindle in Europe.

The First International

Marx remained influential in the Communist movement. His writings inspired the formation of the International Workingman's Party in 1864. The goal of the International, as it was called, was to establish the means for another workers' revolution. Marx eventually became head of the International Workingman's Party. Though Communists established parties all over the world, the International could not get its revolution off the ground.

Communists had some success in France. In 1871, the French government collapsed after losing the Franco-German War. The citizens of Paris elected a radical government. This government set about turning Paris into a commune. In defiance of the national government, the members of which had fled to Versailles, the elected members of the commune began instituting economic and social changes throughout the city. The Commune of Paris outlawed child labor, established a minimum wage, and reopened factories. Communists hailed the Commune of Paris as a first step toward a universal social republic. The French government sent its army to crush the commune. The army attacked on May 21, 1871, and took control of the city on May 28 after a ferocious siege called the Bloody Week. Paris remained under martial law for five years afterward, during which the International Workingman's Party was outlawed.

Soldiers at the Rue Castiglione brace themselves for conflict during the uprising of the French proletariat. Alongside the Prussians, the French recaptured Paris and executed thousands of rebels. Though short-lived, the Commune of Paris gave Communists hope for the future.

Rifts soon appeared in the International. Working conditions in factories had gradually improved. As news of the Commune of Paris's failure sank in, Marx began rethinking the logic of a worldwide revolution. He took greater control of the International and steered it toward a more gradual program of change.

While some followed Marx, others preferred the leadership of Mikhail Bakunin. Bakunin believed strongly in the dissolution of all national governments. He called his movement Revolutionary Socialism. He considered the Communists' new focus on political revolution unreasonable. He and his group, called Anarchists, participated in the congress of the International Workingman's Association in Basel, Switzerland, in 1869. They attempted to steer the congress and therefore the International toward their views, but they were voted down. Bakunin set down the Revolutionary Socialists' agenda in his essay "Marxism, Freedom, and the State," written between 1870 and 1872. He wrote that the Revolutionary Socialists would "organise with a view to the destruction, or if you prefer a politer word, the liquidation of the State."

Bakunin and his followers were kicked out of the International in 1872, but they remained powerful. Feeling increasingly threatened by Bakunin's growing influence, Marx dissolved the International Workingman's Party in 1876. The heads of Communist and Socialist groups still asked his advice, but Marx's days as an organizer were over. He died in 1883.

The Second International

The Communist movement kept progressing despite Marx's clashes with Bakunin. Though governments grew even more hostile toward any type of Communism or Socialism after the bloody fall of the Commune of Paris, Communists continued to organize political parties. In Germany, a Marxist group formed the German Social Democratic Party. The German government responded by making Socialism illegal until 1890. Communists felt the need for a Second International.

ENGELS VERSUS THE ANARCHISTS

Friedrich Engels recognized the threat Bakunin and the Anarchists posed to the Communist movement. In a letter he wrote to Theodor Cuno on January 24, 1872, Engels established the differences between the two ideologies. Anarchism worked to destroy governments, while Communism wished to use them to better the lot of workers until a time when they would become unnecessary.

The Second, or Socialist, International was established in 1889. The German Social Democratic Party and its Russian counterpart dominated the political wing. The Second International's goal was to bring about change within existing systems of government, rather than through violent revolution. Its leaders, including Friedrich Engels, sought to increase the strength of Social Democratic movements.

The Second International began to decline around 1900. The revolutionary elements of the Russian Social Democratic Party agitated against the International's moderate approach. The Second International remained influential until 1914, when many of its members supported their native countries at the onset of World War I. Their patriotism went against the Second International's goal of promoting peace and caused its end.

CHAPTER THREE

THE BOLSHEVIK REVOLUTION

Marx and Engels predicted that the proletarian revolution would begin in an industrialized nation. They reasoned that the revolution needed factories to create the surplus of goods necessary to erase class distinctions. Instead, it happened in Russia, a relatively poor country with a largely agrarian (farm-based) economy and population. Russia's class structure bred enough resentment to spur a revolution.

The Russian Social Democratic Party formed secretly at an 1898 congress in Minsk. At that time, oppressive czars had ruled Russia for centuries. Efforts to

Vladimir Lenin was the first leader of the Soviet Union. He is primarily responsible for transforming Russia into a Communist nation.

ВСЕ СИЛЫ НА ЗАЩИТУ ГОРОДА ЛЕНИНА!

This is a propaganda poster entitled "All Forces to the Defense of the City of Lenin." Socialist realism, a new art movement began under the Soviet government, overwhelmingly depicted factory and construction scenes.

overthrow the czars often resulted in brutal repression.

Lenin's Plan for Revolution

The Russian Social Democratic Party soon felt the pressures of internal conflicts. Its radical members held different views than the more moderate Communists. A fiery young man named Vladimir Ilyich Lenin led the radicals.

Lenin was born Vladimir Ilyich Ulyanov in the city of Simbirsk in 1870. The son of a minor government official, Lenin became interested in radical causes early in life. In 1887, his older brother, Alexandr, was arrested and executed for taking part in a plot to assassinate Czar Alexander III. That year, Lenin distinguished himself for his revolutionary activities at the University of Kazan, where he studied law. He began reading the writings of Karl Marx and absorbing the idea of a workers' revolution.

Lenin practiced law briefly but became a full-time revolutionary by the mid-1890s. The government exiled him to the frigid Siberian countryside in 1895 for organizing workers. He left Russia when his exile ended in 1900, probably adopting the name "Lenin" around this time to disguise his identity while traveling through Europe.

In 1902, Lenin published a pamphlet entitled *What Is to Be Done? Burning Questions of Our Movement*. It outlined his beliefs about how to begin the revolution and create a Communist state. He stated that the proletariat needed outside leadership. It could organize against the bosses and pass labor laws, but it would not be able to bring about a full-scale revolution. The proletariat needed the intellectual community to guide it on the correct path for forming a workers' state.

Lenin recognized the various struggles that had to take place for the Social Democrats to gain power. He wrote, "The political struggle of Social-Democracy is far more extensive and complex than the economic struggle of the workers against the employers and the government." Lenin wanted to form a revolutionary Social Democratic party separate from the workers' groups. Workers should form a broad, public trade union. The revolutionary organization, however, should remain small and secret. Lenin wrote, "The organisation of the revolutionaries must consist first and foremost of people who make revolutionary activity their profession." It would include only trained and experienced revolutionaries, ready to fight the military as the workers seized land and factories.

Bolsheviks and Mensheviks

Lenin presented the ideas of *What Is to Be Done?* at the Second Congress of the Russian Social Democratic Labor Party, held in London in 1903. The party split into two factions. The Bolsheviks (from the Russian word meaning "larger") agreed with Lenin and his views. The Mensheviks (meaning "smaller") wanted to follow a more peaceful route to founding a Communist government. The Bolsheviks gained control of the party.

Though the Russian Social Democratic Labor Party was officially illegal, its members continued to organize workers and spread information about its goals. On January 22, 1905, a group of 200,000 unarmed workers marched to Saint Petersburg's Winter Palace to present a petition to Czar Nicholas II. Guards opened fire on the crowd, killing or wounding hundreds. This massacre began the short Revolution of 1905. Strikes and demonstrations were held all over the country to protest the crackdown. Mutinies occurred in the armed forces. Peasant uprisings took place in the countryside.

Nicholas II tried to calm the Russian citizens. He formed an elected legislative body called the Duma to participate in the government. A general pardon for political exiles allowed Lenin to return to Russia near the end of 1905.

The Fourth Congress of the Russian Social Democratic Labor Party was held in 1906 in Stockholm, Sweden. Party members passed resolutions supporting elections to the Duma. Lenin and the Bolsheviks objected. They wanted nothing short of a total overthrow of Russia's monarchy. Lenin left Russia again in 1907.

Czar Nicholas II gathers the rest of the royal family in the Duma, the lower house of the Russian parliament. Nicholas II was assassinated along with the rest of his family in 1918. He was the last emperor that Russia would ever have.

Strife between the Bolsheviks and the Mensheviks continued. Party membership declined. Lenin and his followers held a conference in 1912. Lenin announced that he was breaking away from the Russian Social Democratic Labor Party to form his own Bolshevik Party.

Last of the Czars

When World War I broke out in 1914, Lenin worked even harder to bring about his revolution. Russia had entered the war on the side of France and Great Britain, pitting it against Germany and

Austria-Hungary. Most Communists and Socialists supported their countries, but Lenin wanted his country to lose the war. He felt Russia's defeat could lead to the revolution he wanted.

Lenin viewed the entire struggle as a war between the world's imperial powers, fighting to extend the reach of capitalism. In his 1916 work *Imperialism, the Highest Stage of Capitalism*, Lenin condemned nations that seized territory belonging to others. He stated that nations fighting in World War I hoped to extend their imperial territory. He claimed that imperialism expanded the wealth and power of the bourgeoisie. This gave them more freedom to exploit and corrupt the proletariat.

Russia's imperial government once again encountered problems in 1917. Rioting broke out in Petrograd (Saint Petersburg) and quickly spread. A committee formed by liberal members of the Duma declared itself the provisional government of Russia. The czar abdicated the throne on March 2, leaving the committee to rule the country.

Petrograd's workers and soldiers also organized a political body. It was called the Petrograd Soviet of Workers' and Soldiers' Deputies. Similar political bodies soon emerged in other Russian cities.

Lenin, in Switzerland, heard about these events. He traveled to Petrograd in early April, ready to further the revolution. Almost immediately upon arrival, he delivered his famous April Theses speech. He called the provisional government "imperialist" and demanded that power should be concentrated in the soviets. He said, "The masses must be made to see that the Soviets of Workers' Deputies are the only possible form of revolutionary government." To Lenin, any other form of government would be too easily corrupted. Lenin proposed that all land be confiscated and used for the public

Under the command of Leon Trotsky, the Red Guard stormed the Winter Palace in Saint Petersburg in 1917. Forty guardsmen captured the palace and arrested the leaders of the provisional government. For the most part, the Red Guard was comprised of working-class civilians.

good; that the police, military, and bureaucracy be disbanded; and that the soviets take over production and distribution of goods.

Soldiers and workers supported the Bolsheviks. On October 6, 1917, the Russian military staged a violent coup, or overthrow of the government, that placed the Bolsheviks in power. They set up a cabinet called the Council of People's Commissars, with Lenin as chairman. Other council members included Leon Trotsky, who organized the coup, and Joseph Stalin. The council immediately abolished private

In this March 19, 1922, letter to members of the Politburo, the main governing committee in the Soviet Union, Lenin outlines a brutal plan to arrest, try, and execute church leaders who were resisting his government's efforts to confiscate church property. Refer to pages 57–58 for a partial transcription.

property and divided private and church lands among the people. Over the next several days, the October Revolution spread to Moscow.

Lenin's long-awaited revolution was tainted. The Bolshevik secret police force, called the Cheka, violently put down opponents. Lenin dissolved councils when Bolsheviks did not have a majority.

The Bolsheviks began negotiating a withdrawal from World War I. In March 1918, Russia accepted the Treaty of Brest-Litovsk. In the treaty, territories that held about a third of Russia's people and cultivated land and most of its industries were given to Germany.

The Bolshevik Party became the Russian Communist Party in March 1918. It faced a major crisis that summer. Russian opposition forces, called the White Army, organized to oust the new government. Leon Trotsky formed an army for the Russian Communist Party called the Red Army. The Russian Civil War ensued. It lasted until 1921. Lenin also responded to the opposition

What Is a Soviet?

A soviet is an elected local committee that is theoretically made up of workers. It serves as a political representative body, similar to a city council. Soviets were created in 1905 under Czar Nicholas II as a way of giving peasants a limited voice in government. Communist revolutionaries used soviets as a way to build opposition to the czarist government.

by beginning the Red Terror. This campaign eliminated political opponents among Russia's citizens. Lenin nationalized factories, instituting strict codes of conduct for the workers. Grain and other crops were seized from the countryside to feed the army and workers in the city. He called these measures War Communism.

The Third International

Lenin organized the Third International, called the Communist International or Comintern, in March 1919. The Third International initially saw Europe as the starting point for the international revolution. It soon switched its attention to Asia, encouraging people living in the colonies to revolt against their European colonizers.

Back in Russia, War Communism was wrecking the economy. Strikes and demonstrations became common. In 1921, Lenin introduced a measure called the New Economic Policy, designed to revitalize the economy. It allowed farmers to sell some of their

Representatives from Germany, Austria-Hungary, and Russia sign the Treaty of Brest-Litovsk. The Russians signed over their control of Finland, Kurland, Livonia, Poland, Ukraine, and what would later be Estonia, Latvia, and Lithuania. The treaty marked the end of Russia's involvement in World War I.

surpluses, lease their land, and put some small businesses back in the hands of private owners.

Lenin suffered a stroke in May 1922. That month, the soviet government established the Union of Soviet Socialist Republics, or USSR. It included Russia and several neighboring countries occupied by the Red Army during the war. Lenin wanted a body of leaders to govern the USSR after his death. He blamed his secretary general, Joseph Stalin, for many of the problems facing the USSR. After Lenin died in January 1924, Stalin emerged as the supreme leader of the Communist Party and the USSR.

CHAPTER FOUR

SOVIET POWER AND ASIAN COMMUNISM

TEORIA E PRÁTICA

J oseph Stalin influenced the policies of the USSR more than any other person. Under his control, the government became an industrial power. Though he brought the government away from the ideas of Marx and Lenin, his form of Communism spread. The international revolution seemed more certain than ever.

Stalin's Rise to Power

Stalin was born Iosif Vissarionovich Dzhugashvili in 1879. The son of a cobbler and a housekeeper, he attended the Tbilisi Theological Seminary in 1894. Stalin also began reading radical

This political cartoon portrays Soviet strongman Joseph Stalin standing on a book by Karl Marx in which several bodies are crushed. Stalin ruled the Soviet Union for nearly thirty years, during which Communism spread around the globe.

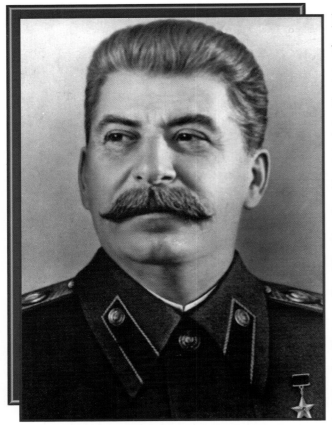

This portrait of Stalin was issued to celebrate his seventieth birthday in 1949. It is believed that Stalin's rough upbringing contributed to his later image of a hardened revolutionary. As a child, Stalin contracted smallpox, which left his face pockmarked. He also had a partially deformed arm.

literature based on Marx's works. He left the seminary in 1899 to devote himself to overthrowing the czar. He joined Lenin's Bolshevik faction in 1903. In 1912, Lenin made him a member of the Bolsheviks' governing Central Committee. By this time, he had adopted the name Stalin, meaning "man of steel" in Russian.

After the October Revolution of 1917, Stalin took an important post in Lenin's council. He headed the Commissariat for Nationality Affairs, which tried to hold together all of the territories of the old Russian Empire. After the Bolsheviks emerged victorious in 1921, Stalin was elected secretary general of the Communist Party. This position put him in charge of appointing officials. Stalin used his new power to place friends within the government and the party. He made sure that other people did not hear of the misgivings Lenin had about him.

Stalin Takes Control

Stalin formed a succession of coalition governments to rule the USSR. His rule faced its toughest trial in 1926, when former partners Lev Kamenev and Grigory Zinovyev joined Stalin's old rival Leon Trotsky to form the Left Opposition. The Left Opposition worked within the party to reduce Stalin's power, but it failed. Stalin forced Trotsky to leave the USSR in 1929. Trotsky's exile signaled the beginning of purges within the party, as Stalin eliminated his opponents.

Stalin abolished Lenin's New Economic Policy in 1928, declaring that it no longer worked. He replaced it with a program called the Five-Year Plan. Stalin designed the plan to bring about rapid industrial growth in Russia. It forced peasants off their land and onto large collective farms, exploiting their labor to help the factories grow. Russia transformed itself into an industrialized nation, but millions starved to death in the process.

The Five-Year Plan brought some benefits to peasants. Russia's literacy rate increased, and the government provided free medical services. The Five-Year Plan was later extended several times.

Controls over daily life became stricter. It became illegal to criticize public policy. Stalin limited the people's freedom of movement. The secret police arrested and executed thousands of party members whom Stalin viewed as potential enemies. These purges increased and spread to the military and civilians. Between 1936 and 1938, the secret police executed more than 1 million people. Some estimates go as high as 7 million. Millions

Taken around 1941, this photograph shows Russian workers from one of Stalin's collective farms with a fresh crop of hay for the Red Army. Their banner reads, "All the harvest for the front."

more were sent to work in forced labor camps. As a result of the "Great Purge," Stalin's officials were loyal to him alone.

Stalin felt that perfection of the USSR would lead to international revolution. To him, democratic measures within the government went against the Communist state's best interests.

World War II

The Nazi Party rose to power in Germany through the 1930s. Stalin publicly supported the Comintern, which opposed Adolf Hitler. He discarded this strategy in 1939, signing the German-Soviet Nonaggression Pact in August of that year. Under the agreement, the USSR allowed Germany to invade Poland. In exchange, Germany promised not to attack Soviet territories.

Hitler broke the pact on June 22, 1941, sending troops into the Soviet Union. The USSR joined the Allied side against Germany, along with Great Britain and the United States. The Soviet army managed to stop Hitler's invasion and drove the Germans out in 1945. The Allies accepted the Nazi surrender on May 7, 1945. The uneasy alliance shared by the USSR and the other Allies soon grew strained. Meanwhile, a Communist revolt had been underway in China for years, led by a man named Mao Tse-tung.

Mao Tse-tung's Rise to Power

Mao Tse-tung was born in 1893. The son of peasants living in China's rural Hunan province, Mao was educated in Chinese literary and philosophical classics. He studied Western philosophy in college. Upon graduating in 1918, he moved to Beijing to work in a library. During this time, he began studying Marxist theory and publishing articles criticizing traditional Chinese values.

Mao traveled to Shanghai in 1921. There, he attended the founding meeting of the Chinese Communist Party (CCP). Mao returned to the

Hunan province and started a branch of the CCP. He began organizing workers' strikes.

The CCP allied itself with the Kuomintang (KMT) party in 1923. The KMT formed in 1912 after a revolution toppled China's imperial government. Its members believed in moderate Socialism. In 1928, KMT leader Chiang Kai-shek launched a violent purge against the CCP.

From 1928 until 1931, Mao and other CCP leaders organized soviets in rural China and built an army. They established a Soviet Republic of China based in the Jiangxi province with Mao as chairman. Mao and his army developed guerilla tactics designed to draw KMT forces into ambushes. Mao and his Red Army continued battling Chiang Kai-shek's KMT army even as Japanese forces attacked China during the Second Sino-Japanese War (1937–1945). The civil war ended in 1949 with China under CCP control. That year, Mao became chairman of the central government committee of the newly formed People's Republic of China.

Mao organized the People's Republic of China based on the example set by the USSR. In 1957, he launched a program called the Great Leap Forward. The plan attempted to industrialize the country without centralizing industrial power. He built thousands of tiny backyard steel mills throughout China and communalized farmlands. Mao intended to produce raw industrial materials throughout the countryside, allowing industries to grow up beside farms.

Mao described the Chinese path to industrialization in his essay "The Correct Handling of Contradictions Among the People":

As China is a large agricultural country, with over 80 percent of her population in the rural areas, industry must develop

敬祝毛主席万寿无疆

This poster, entitled "We Wish Mao a Long Life," pictures Mao Tse-tung in 1968. Image was an important factor of Mao's rule. Pictures of him were almost everywhere. He used propaganda that portrayed him as a sort of savior of the Chinese people. Many thought of him as a god.

万物生长靠太阳

Here, Mao is shown talking to farmers in a cotton field. The poster reads, "The growth of all things depends on the sun." Aspiring to make China as big a producer of goods as Europe and Japan, Mao instituted the Great Leap Forward of 1957.

together with agriculture, for only thus can industry secure raw materials and a market, and only thus is it possible to accumulate fairly large funds for building a heavy industry.

Mao's Great Leap Forward failed miserably. About 20 million people starved in China between 1957 and 1959 as a result of poor planning. The Soviet Union cut off aid following the disaster. Mao gave up his chairmanship of the central government council, but remained chairman of the CCP. He and his supporters launched the Cultural Revolution in 1966. They persecuted Mao's enemies and staged uprisings designed to bring his beliefs back to the fore of China's government. They established a godlike aura around him. All Chinese were encouraged to read Quotations of Chairman Mao, commonly called Mao's Little Red Book. Mao died in 1976, and his followers declared the end of the Cultural Revolution.

CHAPTER FIVE

THE SPREAD OF COMMUNISM

After World War II, the Communist movement appeared to succeed for many years. Mao's revolution in China and the Soviet Union's sponsorship of other Communist movements led to the party's spread throughout Asia and South America. Poor relations with democracies later increased economic problems in Communist countries. Most of these governments fell by the end of the twentieth century.

The Iron Curtain

After the war ended, the Allies divided Germany into four zones, occupied by the USSR, France, the

North Koreans look at a 60-foot-tall statue of Kim Il Sung in central Pyongyang, North Korea, in 1995. Like other Communist dictators, Kim used all types of propaganda to boost his image among his people.

United States, and Britain. They also split Berlin in half. Soon, growing mutual distrust between the United States and the USSR increased tensions. The United States feared that the USSR was trying to expand its territory. When Stalin's troops drove the Nazis from Poland, Stalin set up a Communist-friendly government over objections from the United States.

The Soviets went on to establish Communist governments in other Eastern European countries. (Since then, many of these countries have been reorganized and renamed.) In his 1946 Iron Curtain speech, British prime minister Winston Churchill summed up Europe's anxieties over Stalin's intentions: "A shadow has fallen upon the scenes so lately lighted by the Allied victory. Nobody knows what Soviet Russia and its Communist international organization intends to do in the immediate future, or what are the limits, if any, to their expansive and proselytizing tendencies." Churchill worried that no one knew what the Soviet Union was doing in Eastern Europe. He continued, "An iron curtain has descended across the Continent. Behind that line lie all the capitals of the ancient states of Central and Eastern Europe." By 1948, Stalin had placed Communists in charge of Albania, Yugoslavia, Romania, Bulgaria, Hungary, and Czechoslovakia. The USSR and the countries surrounding it became known as the Soviet bloc.

The United States feared a Communist takeover in the rest of Europe. In 1948, Great Britain, the United States, and France merged their zones to form West Germany. Stalin responded by blockading all the land routes to Berlin, cutting the city's sectors

ALBANIA

Italian forces invaded the Balkan country of Albania in 1939, deposing King Zog I. Albanians formed the Communist-led National Liberation Front (NLF) in 1941 to resist the Italians and the Germans who took their place in 1943. Led by Enver Hoxha, the NLF succeeded in driving German forces out of the country. The NLF changed its name to the Democratic Front and assumed control of the country. Albania held elections in December 1945, with voters choosing from a list of Communist candidates approved by the Democratic Front.

The government adopted a Soviet-style constitution in March 1946 and established the Party of Labour of Albania as the only legal political party. It instituted land reform measures and nationalized businesses. It also developed a close relationship with the Soviet Union. The alliance with the USSR soured, and the Soviets broke off diplomatic ties in 1961. Albania in turn developed ties with Mao Tse-tung's China. Relations with China ended in 1978, bringing isolation and crushing poverty to Albania.

Throughout 1991, anti-Communism demonstrators clamored for a new government. Communism in Albania officially came to an end when free elections were held in March 1992.

off from their national governments. The West launched a massive campaign to airdrop supplies into the city. They broke the blockade after eleven months. By this time, the United States and the USSR viewed each other as threats.

Meanwhile, Stalin and Mao discussed an alliance between their two Communist nations. In December 1949, when China hoped to conquer the island of Formosa (Taiwan), Stalin refused military aid. He said, "Assistance has not been ruled out, though one ought to consider the form of such assistance. What is most important here is not to give Americans a pretext to intervene." The Cold War had begun.

The Cold War

The Cold War was a crisis in international relationships that began after World War II. Tensions between Communist and democratic nations stopped just short of warfare. The United States and the Soviet Union began stockpiling existing weapons and creating new forms of arms. This development became known as the arms race.

U.S. senator Joseph McCarthy captured the Cold War's essence in his famous Wheeling speech delivered in February 1950. "This is a time when all the world is split into two vast, increasingly hostile armed camps—a time of a great armaments race. Today we can almost physically hear the mutterings and rumblings of an invigorated god of war," he said.

Prodded by McCarthy, the United States government took measures against anyone associated with Communism. Small Communist groups had existed in the United States since 1919. Nonetheless, McCarthy believed that they threatened democracy. The House Un-American Activities Committee (HUAC), formed in 1938, investigated suspected Communists through the 1940s and

Senator Joseph McCarthy *(seated, right)* talks to reporters in 1951. During the Red Scare, many people were put on trial. The most famous to be convicted of treason were Ethel and Julius Rosenberg, who were executed in 1953. The Rosenbergs were Americans who were supposedly acting as agents for the Soviet Union.

1950s. People accused of Communist involvement lost their jobs or went to prison, although many were innocent. Senator Joseph McCarthy even accused officials within the U.S. government of being Communists.

The Truman Doctrine of 1947 authorized U.S. support for any nation threatened by Soviet expansion. The United States used the

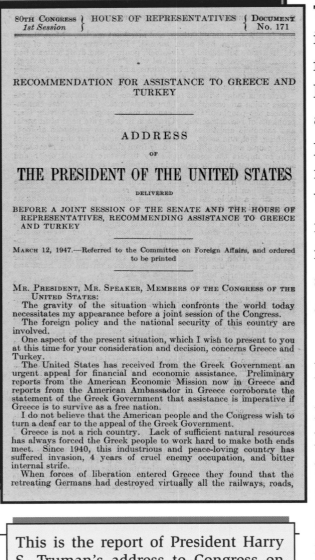

80TH CONGRESS } HOUSE OF REPRESENTATIVES { DOCUMENT
1st Session } { No. 171

RECOMMENDATION FOR ASSISTANCE TO GREECE AND
TURKEY

ADDRESS

OF

THE PRESIDENT OF THE UNITED STATES

DELIVERED

BEFORE A JOINT SESSION OF THE SENATE AND THE HOUSE OF
REPRESENTATIVES, RECOMMENDING ASSISTANCE TO GREECE
AND TURKEY

MARCH 12, 1947.—Referred to the Committee on Foreign Affairs, and ordered
to be printed

MR. PRESIDENT, MR. SPEAKER, MEMBERS OF THE CONGRESS OF THE
UNITED STATES:
The gravity of the situation which confronts the world today
necessitates my appearance before a joint session of the Congress.
The foreign policy and the national security of this country are
involved.
One aspect of the present situation, which I wish to present to you
at this time for your consideration and decision, concerns Greece and
Turkey.
The United States has received from the Greek Government an
urgent appeal for financial and economic assistance. Preliminary
reports from the American Economic Mission now in Greece and
reports from the American Ambassador in Greece corroborate the
statement of the Greek Government that assistance is imperative if
Greece is to survive as a free nation.
I do not believe that the American people and the Congress wish to
turn a deaf ear to the appeal of the Greek Government.
Greece is not a rich country. Lack of sufficient natural resources
has always forced the Greek people to work hard to make both ends
meet. Since 1940, this industrious and peace-loving country has
suffered invasion, 4 years of cruel enemy occupation, and bitter
internal strife.
When forces of liberation entered Greece they found that the
retreating Germans had destroyed virtually all the railways, roads,

This is the report of President Harry S. Truman's address to Congress on March 12, 1947. It became known as the Truman Doctrine. Refer to page 58 for a partial transcription.

Truman Doctrine to justify fighting Mao-supported Communist forces during the Korean War between 1950 and 1953. China and the Soviet Union also supported successful Communist revolutions in Cambodia and Vietnam, despite American involvement in the Vietnam War from 1959 to 1973. Communism soon spread through Central and South America.

North Korea

During World War II, Korea had been occupied by Japan. When the war ended, the United States and the Soviet Union divided the country. The Soviets installed a pro-Communist North Korean Provisional People's Committee in the northern zone in 1946. This body worked on land reform and nationalizing businesses until 1947. That year, it gave way to the Supreme People's Committee, which was selected by voters from a list of Communist-approved candidates. This legislative body in turn chose Kim Il Sung as North Korea's premier in 1948.

Kim attempted to impose Communism on South Korea as well, touching off the Korean War (1950–1953). China offered aid to North Korea, while the United States and other democratic countries supported South Korea. The war ended in a stalemate and further widened the split between the two Koreas. After the war, Kim expanded North Korea's heavy industry and organized the country's agricultural interests around collective farming.

Vietnam

In 1945, the Vietnamese Communist leader Ho Chi Minh (1892–1969) organized the Viet Minh, a league dedicated to winning Vietnam's independence from France. The Viet Minh established the Democratic Republic of Vietnam (DRV), with Ho Chi Minh as president. The French resisted, resulting in the Indo-China War of 1946 to 1954. The signing of the Geneva Accords in 1954 ended the war and split the country into northern and southern halves. Ho Chi Minh became president of the DRV in the Communist-controlled northern half of the country. The southern half, called the Republic of Vietnam (ROV), was governed by an anti-Communist regime.

In 1959, Communist guerillas began attacking targets in South Vietnam, hoping to overthrow its U.S.-supported government. The United States military became involved in 1964 in what would be called the Vietnam War. North Vietnamese forces brought the war to a close in 1975 by capturing Saigon, the South Vietnamese capital.

North Vietnamese president Ho Chi Minh *(second from left)* celebrates the establishment of an interim revolutionary government in South Vietnam on June 14, 1968. The Communist leader ruled North Vietnam for twenty-four years after he declared the country independent in 1945.

They renamed it Ho Chi Minh City and reunified the country as the Socialist Republic of Vietnam in 1976.

Cuba

Fidel Castro led a successful revolution against Cuban dictator General Fulgencio Batista from 1953 to 1959. Castro established a Communist government in Cuba. Led by Dr. Fidel Castro Ruz and the Argentinian-born Dr. Ernesto "Che" Guevara, the revolutionaries seized U.S.-owned businesses without compensating the owners. The United States broke off diplomatic relations and launched the unsuccessful

Fidel Castro *(seated)* and two other Cuban revolutionaries are pictured bearing arms at their Sierra Maestra hideout in Oriente, Cuba, during the Cuban revolution around 1959.

Bay of Pigs invasion in April 1961. Under Castro's guidance, Cuba began a program of radical land reform, nationalized industries, and enacted universal health care. The United States instituted a political and economic blockade against the island nation in 1962. Castro retaliated by strengthening his country's relationship with the USSR.

Cambodia

In 1970, a right-wing faction overthrew the Kingdom of Cambodia's ruler, Prince Norodom Sihanouk, in a bloodless coup. The exiled Prince Sihanouk allied with the Khmer Rouge, a Communist organization, to form the National United Front of Cambodia (FUNC). The ensuing war lasted until 1975, with the FUNC emerging victorious. The country was renamed Kampuchea, and Prince Sihanouk became its head of state. The Khmer Rouge instituted a program to rapidly bring Communism to the country. Money and markets were banned, urban groups were forced into rural areas, and farmlands were rapidly collectivized. As a result, somewhere between 1 and 3 million Cambodians died of famine, disease, and brutality. In 1976, the Khmer Rouge removed Prince Sihanouk from power, replacing him with a guerilla leader named Pol Pot.

CHAPTER SIX

THE DECLINE OF COMMUNISM

Mikhail Gorbachev was the last premier of the Soviet Union. His efforts to keep the union together eventually led to its decline.

S oviet scientists developed an atomic bomb shortly after Stalin's death in 1953. As a result, the arms race between the United States and the Soviet Union escalated.

In 1962, the USSR installed missiles capable of carrying nuclear weapons in Cuba. The Cuban missile crisis caused a panic in the United States. Tense negotiations between the nations followed, ending when the USSR removed the missiles. In exchange, the United States promised not to invade Cuba. In his Universal Conscience speech, delivered in 1968, Castro expressed frustration at being used as a pawn during the crisis. He said, "What really caught our

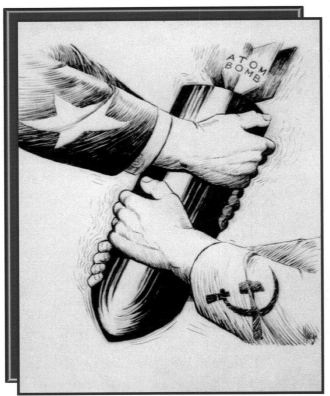

This political cartoon shows two hands holding an atomic bomb. The cartoon paints a symbolic picture of the arms race between the United States and the Soviet Union. There was a great deal of anxiety once both superpowers had atomic weapons capabilities.

attention was the fact that, when peace was truly endangered, when the world was on the brink of a nuclear war, we did not see mass mobilizations in Europe."

The Fall of Communism

Dissatisfaction with Soviet rule became evident in 1968. That year, a reform movement called Prague Spring began in Soviet-controlled Czechoslovakia. Led by intellectuals, it ended censorship and worked toward closer ties with the West. The Soviet Union brutally put down the movement.

The Soviet Union angered the international community in 1979 by invading Afghanistan. The move soured improving relations with the United States. The Soviet economy began to suffer. High prices for natural resource exports kept the USSR's economy afloat through the 1970s, but prices soon fell. No outside markets existed for Soviet manufactured goods. The war in Afghanistan depleted the USSR's cash reserves. The war dragged on until 1989, ending in an embarrassing defeat for the Soviet army.

A family of West Germans look over the Berlin Wall into East Germany in 1962. Construction began on the Berlin Wall on August 13, 1961. The wall was erected to deter immigration between West Germany, which was controlled by Great Britain, France, and the United States, and East Germany, which was controlled by Russia.

Mikhail Gorbachev became general secretary of the USSR in 1985. He began the policies of glasnost (openness) with the media and perestroika (restructuring) within the government and economy. Gorbachev's reforms interrupted the stuttering economy. Shortages became common. Party leaders urged him to slow his reforms.

Gorbachev left the Soviet bloc nations to govern themselves. Many reform governments ousted their Soviet leaders. The most dramatic

This political cartoon, published in 1991, shows Mikhail Gorbachev contemplating a crumbled hammer and sickle (the emblem of the USSR). When Gorbachev was in power, he tried to rescue the Soviet Union from economic decline in the 1980s. However, his efforts didn't stop the superpower's collapse.

instance occurred in Germany. In 1961, the Soviet leader Nikita Khrushchev had ordered a wall built through Berlin. The wall separated the Soviet side of the city from democratic West Berlin. On November 9, 1989, East Germans began tearing down the Berlin Wall.

Gorbachev and the weakened USSR could not stop the independence movements. Vaclav Havel, who was elected president of Czechoslovakia in 1989, announced his views on Communism's decline in a speech given in 1990:

The previous regime—armed with its arrogant and intolerant ideology—reduced man to a force of production and nature to a tool of production. In this it attacked both their very substance and their mutual relationship. It reduced gifted and autonomous people, skillfully working in their own country, to nuts and bolts of some monstrously huge, noisy, and stinking machine, whose real meaning is not clear to anyone. It cannot do more than slowly but inexorably wear down itself and all its nuts and bolts.

A failed coup attempt by members of the military in 1991 marked the end of Gorbachev's reign. He resigned afterward, leaving the government to Boris Yeltsin. Yeltsin dissolved the Communist Party. He and the heads of the Ukraine and Belorussia (Belarus) declared the Soviet Union defunct. All residual functions of the Soviet Union stopped on December 31, 1991. The USSR faded out of existence.

Communism Today

Since the Soviet Union's fall, few Communist countries have remained. The People's Republic of China, North Korea, Vietnam, and Cuba make up the list of surviving Communist governments. Communist parties still thrive across the globe, though their objective has changed. Most no longer reach for a worldwide revolution. Instead, they form coalition parties with other liberal groups and work for causes they believe in. Despite the stigma attached to Communist governments by the policies of Stalin and Mao, many are still willing to answer Marx's rallying call for workers of all countries to unite.

TIMELINE

375 BC	Plato completes *Republic*.
1516	Thomas More publishes his influential book *Utopia*.
1799	Robert Owen buys several mills in New Lanmark, Scotland, and begins building utopian communities.
1847	The Communist League commissions Karl Marx and Friedrich Engels to write *The Communist Manifesto*.
1871	The French army puts down the Commune of Paris.
1905	The Revolution of 1905 begins in Russia.
1917	Vlaldimir Lenin overthrows Russia's government and installs the world's first Communist national government.
1922	The Union of Soviet Socialist Republics (USSR) is founded.
1924	Joseph Stalin assumes control of the USSR.
1928	Stalin implements the Five-Year Plan.
1931	Mao Tse-tung begins a Communist uprising in China.
1953	Soviet scientists develop the atomic bomb.
1959	Fidel Castro's Communist movement overthrows the Cuban government.
1961	The Soviet Union builds the Berlin Wall, dividing East from West Berlin.
1962	The Cuban missile crisis takes place.
1968	The Soviet army invades Czechoslovakia to end the Prague Spring movement.
1985	Mikhail Gorbachev becomes general secretary of the USSR.
1989	East Germans tear down the Berlin Wall.
1991	The USSR is officially declared defunct.

Page 16: Excerpt from *The Communist Manifesto*

A specter is haunting Europe—the specter of communism. All the powers of old Europe have entered into a holy alliance to exorcise this specter . . .

But whatever form they may have taken, one fact is common to all past ages, viz., the exploitation of one part of society by the other. No wonder, then, that the social consciousness of past ages, despite all the multiplicity and variety it displays, moves within certain common forms, or general ideas, which cannot completely vanish except with the total disappearance of class antagonisms . . .

In short, the Communists everywhere support every revolutionary movement against the existing social and political order of things.

In all these movements they bring to the front, as the leading question in each case, the property question, no matter what its degree of development at the time.

Finally, they labor everywhere for the union and agreement of the democratic parties of all countries.

The Communists disdain to conceal their views and aims. They openly declare that their ends can be attained only by the forcible overthrow of all existing social conditions. Let the ruling classes tremble at a Communist revolution. The proletarians have nothing to lose but their chains. They have a world to win.

Workingmen of all countries, unite!

Page 30: March 19, 1922, letter from Lenin to members of the Politburo

Copy To Comrade Molotov

Top Secret For members of the Politburo

Please make no copies for any reason. Each member of the Politburo (incl. Comrade Kalinin) should comment directly on the document.

We must pursue the removal of church property by any means necessary in order to secure for ourselves a fund of several hundred million gold rubles (do not forget the immense wealth of some monasteries and lauras). . . But to do this successfully is possible only now. All considerations indicate that later on we will fail to do this, for no other time, besides that of desperate famine, will give us such a mood among the general mass of peasants that would ensure us the sympathy of this group, or, at least, would ensure us the neutralization of this group in the sense that victory in the struggle for the removal of church property unquestionably and completely will be on our side. . .

Therefore, I come to the indisputable conclusion that we must precisely now smash the Black Hundreds clergy most decisively and ruthlessly and put down all resistance with such brutality that they will not forget it for several decades . . .

Lenin.

Page 46: Excerpt from the Truman Doctrine

At the present moment in world history nearly every nation must choose between alternative ways of life. The choice is too often not a free one.

One way of life is based upon the will of the majority, and is distinguished by free institutions, representative government, free elections, guaranties of individual liberty, freedom of speech and religion, and freedom from political oppression.

The second way of life is based upon the will of a minority forcibly imposed upon the majority. It relies upon terror and oppression, a controlled press and radio, fixed elections, and the suppression of personal freedoms.

I believe that it must be the policy of the United States to support free peoples who are resisting attempted subjugation by armed minorities or by outside pressures. I believe that we must assist free peoples to work out their own destinies in their own way. I believe that our help should be primarily through economic and financial aid which is essential to economic stability and orderly political processes . . .

Should we fail to aid Greece and Turkey in this fateful hour, the effect will be far-reaching to the West as well as to the East. We must take immediate and resolute action.

I therefore ask the Congress to provide authority for assistance to Greece and Turkey in the amount of $400,000,000 for the period ending June 30, 1948. In requesting these funds, l have taken into consideration the maximum amount of relief assistance which would be furnished to Greece out of the $350,000,000 which I recently requested that the Congress authorize for the prevention of starvation and suffering in countries devastated by the war.

GLOSSARY

ambassador A diplomat who represents his or her country's government while dealing with other nations.

arms race A competition between nations to have the most powerful stock of weapons.

bloc A combination of nations with common interests.

capital A part of the proceeds of industry, which can either support human beings or assist in production.

capitalist One who practices capitalism, the economic system based on private and corporate ownership of goods and business rather than state control.

colonization A country's practice of sending out groups of people to live and work in territory outside of their home nation.

commentary A record or explanation of events.

communal Shared by members of a community; especially when property is collectively owned.

cornerstone A basic element, or foundation, of a policy.

czar A monarch who ruled the Russian Empire before the October Revolution of 1917. Also spelled "tsar."

exploitation Improper use of another person or group for selfish purposes.

idealistic Placing beliefs before practical considerations.

imperial Relating to or describing an empire.

labor union A group organized by workers to improve members' wages, benefits, and working conditions.

opportunism The practice of taking advantage of circumstances with little regard for principles or consequences.

servitude The condition of being bound to service, or a lack of personal freedom.

soviet An elected government council in a Communist country.

specter A ghost, or something that haunts the mind. The British spelling is "spectre."

wages Payment for labor, usually on an hourly or daily basis.

FOR MORE INFORMATION

Web Sites

Due to the changing nature of Internet links, the Rosen Publishing Group, Inc., has developed an online list of Web sites related to the subject of this book. This site is updated regularly. Please use this link to access the list:

http://www.rosenlinks.com/psps/comm

FOR FURTHER READING

Allan, Tony. *The Long March: The Making of Communist China.* Chicago: Heinemann Library, 2001.

Cipkowski, Peter. *Revolution in Eastern Europe: Understanding the Collapse of Communism in Poland, Hungary, East Germany, Czechoslovakia, Romania and the Soviet Union.* New York: John Wiley & Sons, 1991.

Edwards, Judith. *Lenin and the Russian Revolution in World History.* Berkeley Heights, NJ: Enslow Publishers, Inc., 2001.

Ingram, Scott. *Joseph Stalin.* Woodbridge, CT: Blackbirch Marketing, 2002.

Kettle, Arnold. *Karl Marx: Founder of Modern Communism.* New York: Roy Publishers, 1964.

McAleavy, Tony. *Superpower Rivalry: The Cold War.* New York: SIGS Books & Multimedia, 1998.

BIBLIOGRAPHY

Borkenau, Franz. *World Communism*. Ann Arbor, MI: University of Michigan Press, 1978.

Hobsbawm, Eric. *The Age of Extremes: A History of the World, 1914–1991*. New York: Pantheon Books, 1994.

Oglesby, Carl, ed. *The New Left Reader*. New York: Grove Press, Inc., 1969.

Owen, Robert. *A New View of Society and Other Writings*. New York: Penguin Books, 1991.

Ozinga, James R. *Communism: The Story of the Idea and its Implementation*. Englewood Cliffs, NJ: Prentice-Hall, Inc., 1987.

Schrecker, Ellen. *The Age of McCarthyism: A Brief History with Documents*. New York: St. Martin's Press, 1994.

Trotsky, Leon. *The First 5 Years of the Communist International, Vol. 1*. New York: Pathfinder Press, 1972.

Tse-tung, Mao. *Four Essays on Philosophy*. Peking (Beijing), China: Foreign Languages Press, 1968.

Tucker, Robert C., ed. *The Marx-Engels Reader*. New York: W. W. Norton and Company, 1978.

PRIMARY SOURCE IMAGE LIST

Cover: Photograph of Vladimir Lenin addressing audience in St. Petersburg, Russia, in March 1917.

Pages 4–5: Photograph of Chairman Mao Tse-tung reviewing Russian troops during a 1957 trip to Russia.

Page 6: Engraving of Robert Owen, circa 1810.

Page 9: *The Island of Utopia*, woodcut by Ambrosius Holbein, circa 1517.

Page 12: Socialist Labor Party poster, bearing an image of Karl Marx. Created and published between 1965 and 1980. Housed at the Library of Congress Prints and Photographs Division in Washington, D.C.

Page 14 (left): Portrait of Karl Marx. Housed at the Library of Congress Prints and Photographs Division in Washington, D.C.

Page 14 (right): Portrait of Friedrich Engels. Housed at the Library of Congress Prints and Photographs Division in Washington, D.C.

Page 16: Cover of the first authorized English translation of *The Communist Manifesto* by Karl Marx and Friedrich Engels. Housed at the Karl Marx House in Trier, Germany.

Page 24: "All Forces to the Defense of the City of Lenin," poster created by Dementii Alekseevich Shmarinov in 1970. Housed at the Library of Congress Prints and Photographs Division in Washington, D.C.

Page 27: Photograph of Czar Nicholas II opening the Russian Duma around 1916.

Page 29: Photograph of the Red Guard attacking the Winter Palace in St. Petersburg, Russia, in October 1917.

Page 30: March 19, 1922, letter from Lenin to members of the Politburo. Housed at the Library of Congress in Washington, D.C.

Page 32: Photograph of the signing of the Treaty of Brest-Litovsk on March 3, 1918.

Page 33: Political cartoon depicting Joseph Stalin using one of Karl Marx's books to crush people. Housed at the Library of Congress Prints and Photographs Division in Washington, D.C.

Page 34: Photograph of Soviet premier Joseph Stalin, 1949.

Page 36: Photograph of collective farm workers near Moscow, Russia, circa 1941. Housed at the Library of Congress Prints and Photographs Division in Washington, D.C.

Page 39: Poster showing portrait of Mao Tse-tung within a rising sun, 1968. Housed at the Library of Congress Prints and Photographs Division in Washington, D.C.

Page 40: Poster showing Mao Tse-tung talking to farmers, circa 1970. Housed at the Library of Congress Prints and Photographs Division in Washington, D.C.

Page 45: Photograph of Senator Joseph McCarthy talking to reporters in 1951. Housed at the Library of Congress in Washington, D.C.

Page 46: Page from President Harry Truman's speech to Congress on February 21, 1947. Housed at the Harry S. Truman Library in Independence, Missouri.

Page 48: Photograph of Ho Chi Minh at a political rally in South Vietnam, in 1968.

Page 49: Photograph of an armed Fidel Castro, circa 1960. Housed at the Library of Congress in Washington, D.C.

Page 51: Photograph of Soviet president Mikhail Gorbachev, February 1, 1990.

Page 52: Political cartoon portraying the United States and the Soviet Union grasping for an atom bomb. Created around 1949 by Edwin Marcus. Housed at the Library of Congress Prints and Photographs Division in Washington, D.C.

Page 53: Photograph of a group of West Germans looking over the Berlin Wall in 1962. Housed at the Library of Congress Prints and Photographs Division in Washington, D.C.

Page 54: Political cartoon portraying Mikhail Gorbachev watching over the disintegration of the Soviet Union. Created by Edmund S. Valtman in 1991. Housed at the Library of Congress Prints and Photographs Division in Washington, D.C.

INDEX

PHOTO CREDITS

Cover © Voller Ernst/eStock Photo; back cover (top left) NARA; back cover (all others) © The 2000 Nova Corporation; pp. 1, 12, 14, 24, 33, 36, 39, 40, 49, 52, 53, 54 © Library of Congress Prints and Photographs Division; pp. 4–5, 6, 9, 20, 27 © Hulton/Archive/Getty Images; p. 8 © Bridgeman Art Library, London/Superstock; p. 16 © Friedrich Ebert Foundation/The Karl Marx House; p. 23 © SuperStock; p. 29 © Keystone/Hulton/Archive/Getty Images; p. 30 © Library of Congress; p. 32 © Topical Press Agency/Hulton/Archive/Getty Images; pp. 34, 48 © AP/Wide World Photos; p. 41 © John Leicester/AP/Wide World Photos; p. 45 © New York World-Telegram & Sun Collection (LOC); p. 46 © Harry S. Truman Library and Museum/NARA; p. 51 © Sergei Guneyev/Time Life Pictures/Getty Images.

ABOUT THE AUTHOR

Theodore Link is a freelance writer who lives in Chicago, Illinois.

Designer: Evelyn Horovicz; **Editor:** Wayne Anderson;
Photo Researcher: Hillary Arnold